Microsoft
OneDrive 2024

Exploring the advanced features of Microsoft OneDrive in the Business World. Save and secure your document in the cloud, scan it with your mobile phone, and a lot more.

BY:

NELSON TURNER

CONTENTS

INTRODUCTION

Embark on an exploration of the expansive realm of Microsoft OneDrive with this user-friendly guide tailored for 2024. Whether you're a newcomer to cloud storage or seeking to unlock the advanced features of OneDrive, this guide presents a step-by-step roadmap. Covering fundamental tasks such as basic uploads, seamless integration with Microsoft Office, and delving into advanced business functionalities, each aspect of OneDrive is elucidated for a comprehensive understanding. Rich with comparisons against counterparts like Google Drive and SharePoint, this guide offers a well-rounded perspective. With a dedicated emphasis on security measures and strategies for business optimization, it ensures that you are well-prepared to harness the full potential of OneDrive. Embrace the future of digital storage and collaboration with confidence through this insightful guide.

In this book, chapter one focuses on the OneDrive desktop user interface which will enable users to customize folder colors, offering a visual cue to expedite the identification of folder contents.

It also focuses on OneDrive with Copilot Integration and being assisted by AI in finding folders, and also talks about you setting up your account with Microsoft OneDrive, collaboration on OneDrive, and synchronizing OneDrive with your business.

Chapter two explains the main features of OneDrive 2024 and the expected features of OneDrive etc.

CHAPTER ONE

UNDERSTANDING OneDrive

WHAT EXACTLY IS OneDrive

Microsoft OneDrive, commonly known as just OneDrive, is a cloud computing service designed to facilitate the uploading and synchronization of files to cloud storage. This allows users to access their files through a designated web browser or compatible device. Similar to services like Dropbox and Google Drive, OneDrive offers seamless integration with the user's computer.

The Application folder can be automatically synchronized between OneDrive and the user's computer. This enables users to work on documents even when offline. The service synchronizes data across computers, phones, and/or tablets, provided they are linked to the same Microsoft account. When connected to the network, any modifications made to files are automatically updated in the user's OneDrive storage area on the Internet.

KEY FEATURES AND ADVANTAGES

OneDrive boasts an appealing web and mobile interface, offering music downloads, functioning as a smart photo repository, supporting real-time co-editing, and providing enhanced search capabilities. Its seamless integration with Windows 10 and Office 365 further enhances its functionality.

Aligning with other cloud storage services, OneDrive offers a range of features. It serves as a virtual USB hard drive, storing files that are easily accessible from the web. Additionally, it facilitates directory sync to aggregate files from various PCs. For Windows 10 users, it efficiently backs up machine settings, encompassing the lock screen, wallpaper, and web browser favorites. OneDrive also synchronizes Office files and offers a co-authoring mode.

Given its diverse features and robust support across multiple devices and platforms, the layout and arrangement of features may vary depending on the device in use. OneDrive accommodates a broad spectrum of file types, spanning from standard office files to multimedia files. The traditional distinction between cloud storage and conventional storage devices is virtually eliminated.

Microsoft's cloud storage service accommodates a wide array of common file types, with specific details for each type outlined below:

Document: For those familiar with iCloud's web interface, Onedrive's file viewing and editing capabilities are easily navigable, thanks to its built-in Office integration. Document files support real-time collaborative editing, allowing multiple individuals to edit simultaneously— a feature also recognized by Google Drive users.

Music and Sound: File types are no longer a hindrance; you can directly listen to audio files on Onedrive without the need for downloading. However, its web version currently does not support lossless FLAC music files. For this, you may consider installing Win 10's Groove app.

Photos and Videos: Onedrive's web interface offers an excellent display of picture files, with functionalities such as labeling, grouping, and object identification comparable to Flickr. Its searchability is on par with Google Photos, a feature lacking in iCloud. Sharing photos and tagging oneself in pictures can be done without requiring a Microsoft account. Naturally, it includes decentralized features like read-only or editorial permissions. When sharing videos, all data is compressed in MPEG-DASH format, accommodating various bandwidth speeds.

Extracting Text from Images: A notable feature is the ability to extract text from images, known as OCR (Optical Character Recognition). Onedrive's information panel for shapes displays text, facilitating easy copy and paste. This feature sets Onedrive apart, as Google Drive, iCloud, and Dropbox have yet to incorporate it.

GETTING FAMILIAR WITH THE ONEDRIVE DESKTOP USER INTERFACE

Microsoft has introduced the latest iteration of OneDrive, featuring an array of new functionalities crafted to streamline file management for both business and home users, fostering enhanced efficiency and collaboration. OneDrive 3.0 encompasses a revamped home screen integrating Copilot, AI-driven recommendations, offline web syncing, improved sharing and collaboration capabilities, and more. These enhancements aim to elevate the file management experience across web platforms, applications, and Windows 11.

While certain features and modifications are currently being rolled out, a more extensive set is anticipated to be available in December. Notably, features like Copilot are slated for release in 2024. As part of this update, Microsoft is overhauling the web interface of OneDrive, introducing a fresh design that aligns seamlessly with the design language present in Windows 11, Microsoft 365 applications, and File Explorer.

OneDrive New Interface

OneDrive's updated interface introduces a dynamic "Home" page featuring the "For You" section, leveraging AI to suggest and prioritize relevant files from OneDrive, Teams, or other sources. The left navigation now incorporates context-based organization, offering views such as shared, favorites, people, and meetings for convenient file browsing.

A prominent "Add New" button expedites the creation of files and folders, enabling direct content uploads from your computer. The "Shared" page compiles files shared via Teams, emails, and other Office documents, including a new "Activity" inline view to track pertinent comments. Microsoft is also simplifying file permission management.

The "Favorites" page is dedicated to files marked as favorites, now achievable with the "start-tap" option. Furthermore, you can include "File Shortcut" links within existing OneDrive folders. Notably, favorite files can seamlessly roam across devices and the web, ensuring accessibility across various platforms.

Among the notable updates is the ability for favorite files to sync across OneDrive on different devices and the web. For instance, marking a file as a favorite on the web mirrors the same designation in the "Favorites" section of File Explorer on Windows 11.

The "People" page categorizes files based on collaborators, facilitating easier file retrieval based on project collaborators. Users can pin individuals at the top of the page, streamlining file activities without the need to open each file individually.

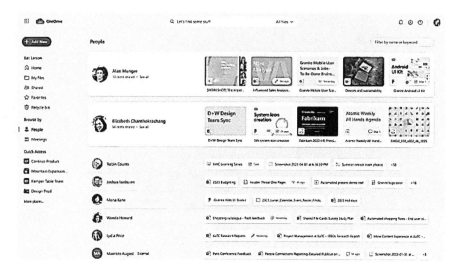

In the latest iteration of OneDrive, users now have the option to customize folder colors, offering a visual cue to expedite the identification of folder contents.

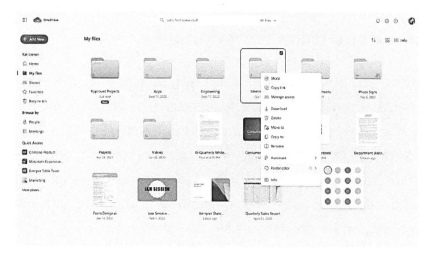

The "Meetings" page categorizes content based on what has been shared during meetings, encompassing chats, notes, and loops. Additionally, users invited to upcoming meetings gain early access to associated files.

Microsoft is also in the works to introduce a new "Media" view. This feature will enable users to centralize their images, videos, and media in a single location, facilitating visual browsing of content within this dedicated space.

Browser Offline Functionality

Offline support is a significant enhancement in the new version of OneDrive, enabling users to access OneDrive in the browser even without an internet connection. Additionally, Files On-Demand will be introduced in the browser, allowing users to designate specific files for offline availability. OneDrive 3.0 promises faster loading times, doubling its speed, and delivering immediate sorting, enhanced scrolling, and more responsive performance.

Another upcoming feature is the ability to open files directly from cloud storage on the web into their respective native desktop applications, bypassing the need to use web versions. Microsoft is extending this functionality to include opening CAD and PDF files, in addition to Word, Excel, PowerPoint, and other formats.

As part of business integration, the enhanced OneDrive experience is slated to be seamlessly integrated into the files section of Microsoft Teams and Outlook.

OneDrive with Copilot Integration

Microsoft is also integrating its AI capabilities into OneDrive with the introduction of Copilot.

Initially launched with the Windows 11 Copilot update, this feature is now extended to OneDrive. While it is assumed that Copilot will be available for both business and consumer versions of OneDrive, the official announcement specifies availability for customers with a Microsoft 365 Copilot license and Microsoft 365 Chat subscription.

Furthermore, AI improvements extend to the search experience in OneDrive. Significant changes aim to enhance file discovery through more accurate keyword searches, file type categorization, and personalized suggestions based on search history. The "Home" page now includes filters for quick sorting of Word, Excel, PowerPoint, and PDF files.

While some features and changes are currently rolling out, others are anticipated in the coming months. The "Add New" feature is expected in the summer of 2024, and the Copilot feature will be available in public preview in early 2024 (with a limited chatbot preview in December). Offline support, Files On demand, and the ability to open files with desktop apps from the web will be introduced in 2024. The "Media" view is set to debut in the summer of 2024.

Setting Up Your Account With Onedrive

To initiate OneDrive, launch your web browser and visit the following website:

onedrive.com

To begin, you'll need to create an account. If you already possess a Microsoft account, you can utilize it to log in to OneDrive.

If not, click on 'Create free account' and follow the prompts to enter your details.

Navigating the OneDrive Interface

The OneDrive interface is user-friendly. Upon signing in, your files and folders will be displayed either as a list or as icons. You can create new items by clicking the "New" button, or you can upload files to OneDrive using the upload button. The search bar at the top of the screen allows you to search for specific files and folders.

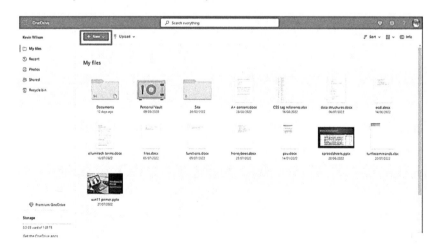

OneDrive features a sidebar on the left-hand side. Click on the 'my files' link to view all files saved to OneDrive. Other links include Recent Files, Photos, Shared Files, and the Recycle bin. The 'Shared' link displays files and folders shared with you, while 'Recent' shows items accessed recently. 'Photos' provides a shortcut to your photo albums, and 'Recycle bin' reveals deleted files and folders.

Uploading Files

Uploading files to OneDrive is a straightforward process. Click "Upload," then choose the file on your device or PC for upload. Alternatively, you can drag and drop files directly into the OneDrive window.

Generate a New File

To initiate a new file, select 'new,' and then pick the file type from the dropdown menu. Options include Word documents, Excel spreadsheets, PowerPoint presentations, and others. This action will launch the new file in the respective online application version: Word, Excel, PowerPoint, etc.

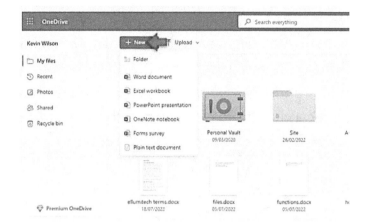

Once the file opens, click on the document name at the top. In the dropdown menu, provide a meaningful name for the document.

Now, you can commence working on your file.

Collaboration on OneDrive

OneDrive simplifies collaboration on documents, presentations, and spreadsheets. Utilize the "Share" button located at the top right of the screen to share files with others.

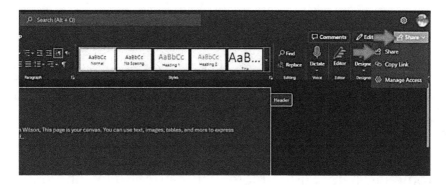

Sign in with the Microsoft account of the individual you wish to share the file with. This action will dispatch a link that they can click on.

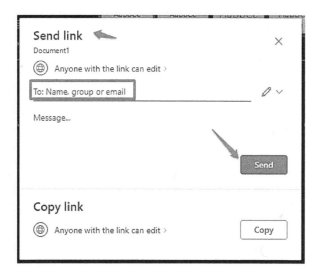

When you share a file, the other individual can simultaneously edit the file with you, facilitating collaboration on projects regardless of your location.

Synchronizing OneDrive with Your Devices

OneDrive is seamlessly integrated into Windows 10/11 and appears in File Explorer upon signing in. Additionally, you can download the OneDrive app for Mac, iPhone, iPad, and Android devices. Locate the app in the respective device's App Store.

One of the notable advantages of OneDrive is its seamless synchronization with your devices. Any modifications made to a file on one device will be automatically reflected on all your other devices. To sync OneDrive with your devices, download the OneDrive app and sign in with your Microsoft account.

Once OneDrive is synced with your device, you can access your files from anywhere. Furthermore, you can edit files on your device and then sync them back to OneDrive.

CHAPTER TWO

THE MOST-REQUESTED FEATURES ON ONEDRIVE VS NEW FEATURES

Microsoft's OneDrive, an integrated file syncing and hosting service within the Windows operating system, is accessible across various platforms, with open registration for anyone interested. Over the years, the service has undergone multiple iterations, introducing new apps, designs, and features, and occasionally retiring some.

Users are encouraged to provide feedback and suggestions through Microsoft's Feedback Portal, with the company addressing the most requested features. Here are the top 10 OneDrive features that users have tagged as open, with insights from Microsoft:

Ignore or Exclude Folders from Sync
- User Request: Allow excluding selected OneDrive folders from the sync process.
- Microsoft's Response: The company plans to expand the file exclusion feature to folders.

Enable Syncing over LAN
- User Request: Enable syncing between devices on the same local network without internet connectivity.
- Microsoft's Response: This feature is under consideration, but there's no specific timeline yet.

Store Shared Folders within Subfolders
- User Request: Allow shared folders to be stored within subfolders for better organization.
- Microsoft's Response: Microsoft is actively working on adding this functionality.

Implement a Folder Tree

- User Request: Introduce a folder tree structure for improved navigation and file management.
- Microsoft's Response: This feature is part of the future roadmap.

Enable Linux Support

- User Request: Provide an official OneDrive client for Linux.
- Microsoft's Response: No official response was provided.

People Tagging Feature

- User Request: Add a people tagging feature and facial recognition support for automated tagging.
- Microsoft's Response: Planned, but no specific timeline available.

Rename OneDrive for Business Folders

- User Request: Allow renaming OneDrive for Business folders.
- Microsoft's Response: Noted by the company.

Access Personal Vault via MacOS

- User Request: Enable access to the Personal Vault on Macs through the OneDrive for Mac clients.
- Microsoft's Response: No official response was provided.

Zip and Unzip Files in Web Version

- User Request: Add an option to zip or unzip files directly in the web version of OneDrive.
- Microsoft's Response: Under consideration for future updates.

Prevent the Download of Shared Files

- User Request: Provide an option to prevent shared files from being downloaded.
- Microsoft's Response: Implemented for certain file types (PDFs, images, audio) with plans to extend support to other types in the future.

These feature requests and Microsoft's responses offer insights into the ongoing evolution of OneDrive, addressing user needs and enhancing the overall user experience.

MAIN FEATURES OF MICROSOFT ONEDRIVE 2024

OneDrive has undergone significant development since its initial launch as a cloud storage provider. It has evolved to become the central hub for file management within Microsoft 365. Going beyond mere storage, OneDrive now facilitates file sharing, collaboration, and robust security features, catering to individuals and organizations of all sizes worldwide. With trillions of hosted files and an addition of nearly 2 billion files daily, OneDrive has become an integral part of digital workflows.

As the professional landscape transforms, OneDrive is adapting to align with your evolving needs. Presently, your work files extend across OneDrive, and SharePoint document libraries, attachments in meeting invites, and exchanges through Teams chats. The challenge lies in having a unified space where you can effortlessly locate all your files, Loops, dashboards, and design boards, regardless of their location. Today, we are excited to introduce the next generation of OneDrive, placing all your files at your fingertips.

The enhanced OneDrive experience features new file views, governance controls, creation tools, and the introduction of Copilot, designed to streamline your ability to search, organize, and extract information from your files. These improvements extend beyond OneDrive; they are seamlessly integrated into Teams and Outlook, providing a consistent and enriched file experience throughout the Microsoft 365 ecosystem. Let's explore the advancements in the next generation of OneDrive.

Onedrive Copilot

Leveraging Microsoft 365 Chat, users can harness Copilot's AI capabilities for comprehensive integration with all Microsoft 365 data, encompassing files from both OneDrive and SharePoint.

In anticipation of future developments, Microsoft is actively enhancing Copilot with new skills to further streamline organization on OneDrive. A notable upcoming feature involves Copilot's ability to autonomously generate new folders based on file search criteria.

Additionally, Moore highlights that Copilot is poised to accelerate the processes of gathering, managing, and transferring knowledge, offering users a faster and more efficient experience.

To ensure a consistent user experience, these forthcoming updates will extend to Teams and Outlook, providing seamless integration across the Microsoft 365 platform, as outlined by Moore.

Copilot in Excel: Enhancing Productivity in 4 Ways with AI

Leveraging Copilot in Excel goes beyond conventional data management, offering four impactful ways to significantly boost your productivity.

- Copilot acts as a reliable assistant, aiding you in gaining a deeper understanding of your data. Its intuitive capabilities allow for effortless comprehension, providing valuable insights to unravel the intricacies of your datasets.
- With Copilot, the process of creating tables and charts is streamlined, offering you dynamic visual representations of your data. This feature enables you to gain fresh perspectives, making

it easier to interpret and communicate complex information effectively.

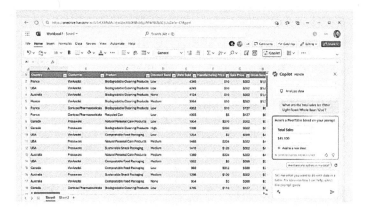

- By analyzing your Excel data, Copilot generates insightful observations, unlocking opportunities for further exploration. For instance, it can present various sums that offer valuable insights into budgetary considerations, empowering you with informed decision-making.
- Copilot goes beyond mere data analysis; it actively assists you in exploring your datasets. Its capabilities extend to proposing meaningful insights, guiding you through the exploration process and enhancing your overall data-driven decision-making.

Copilot in Excel serves as a powerful tool, revolutionizing the way you interact with and derive insights from your data. Whether it's creating visual representations or uncovering hidden patterns, Copilot seamlessly integrates AI assistance into your Excel workflow, enhancing your productivity and analytical capabilities.

File Management Enhancements

OneDrive for work and school is set to provide more streamlined access to your files through a revamped home experience, AI-driven file suggestions, and a meetings overview highlighting upcoming and past meetings along with associated recordings and shared files.

Introducing a 'people view,' the platform will organize files based on individuals who shared them with you, while a 'shared view' will present a dedicated display of shared files.

Additional file access features encompass a list of favorite files, shortcuts, and simplified sharing processes, aiming to reduce the number of clicks required for efficient navigation and utilization.

File Organization, Access, and Creation

The "Open in app" feature empowers users to open any file in its desktop app, make edits, and seamlessly synchronize the changes.

An update to the Files app in Teams incorporates the OneDrive Teams app, providing comprehensive access to files across SharePoint and OneDrive directly from Teams.

OneDrive app is integrated into the left navigation of Outlook for Windows and Outlook on the web, simplifying tasks like copying and sharing links.

The 'Sync' functionality is expanding to the browser experience, allowing offline files to be locally available from OneDrive for the web. Any modifications made in offline mode in the web browser will automatically sync to OneDrive once an internet connection is re-established.

The introduction of 'media view' will enable users to consolidate images, videos, and media into a single location, facilitating visual content exploration.

Additionally, the public preview release of new AI search features for consumers. These features will enable users to locate photos based on criteria such as person, place, or specific objects, using natural language search.

Security and Governance

Microsoft has introduced a suite of security and governance features to enhance OneDrive.

These include granular conditional access policies, restricted access control on files, simplified migration of OneDrive accounts across tenants, the capability to block file downloads, and collaboration insights to identify sharing patterns and user collaborations.

CHAPTER THREE

SYNCING FILES IN ONEDRIVE

Microsoft OneDrive offers complimentary online storage to its users. By utilizing OneDrive, you can effortlessly synchronize your files between your PC and the cloud, enabling you to work with your files seamlessly while on the move!

Once you synchronize with Microsoft OneDrive, you gain the capability to reach your files from any device—be it a computer, mobile phone, or tablet—using your Microsoft Account. Any additions, modifications, or deletions made to files or folders within your OneDrive folder will be automatically mirrored on the OneDrive website, and vice versa.

EXPLORE ONEDRIVE ON YOUR COMPUTER AND IN THE CLOUD

To begin, launch OneDrive on your computer and access it online. Below, you'll find depictions of OneDrive's appearance on a PC (left side) and its online interface (right side).

In both instances, a folder named "Demo" is present. You can initiate a single-click action on this folder in the cloud or double-click on the PC to open it.

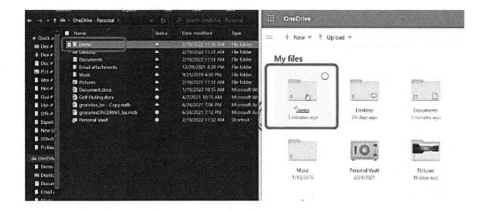

You may have observed that the files present in the cloud are identical to those on the PC.

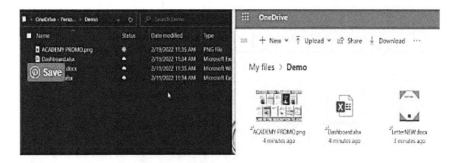

Icons for File and Folder Level Synchronization

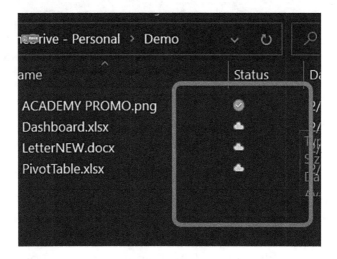

Within this OneDrive folder, there are two distinct icons – a Green icon and a Cloud icon.

Let's examine the significance of both these icons:

- **Green Icon:** This icon features a green circle with a white checkmark. Files marked with this icon are designated as "Always keep on this device." This implies that these files exist both in the folder on your computer and in the cloud.
- **Cloud Icon:** This icon is a blue-outlined cloud symbol adjacent to the file. It signifies that the file is exclusively available online and does not occupy space on your computer. When you access this file, you are essentially opening the version stored in the cloud. If you lack access to the cloud, this file will not open.

These icons represent file-level synchronization. Now, let's delve into how the folder-level syncing icon operates!

Here, you'll notice that the Demo folder is adorned with a cloud icon, signifying the presence of at least one file in this folder that is stored in the cloud.

Altering Microsoft OneDrive Sync Status

To access the files within the Demo folder, a single click will suffice. Now, let's attempt to modify the sync icon from the cloud to a green checkmark, indicating the intention to keep the file both on the PC and in the cloud.

1. Right-click on the file.
2. Select "Always keep on this device."

Now, go back to the **Demo folder** and check the **syncing icon.**

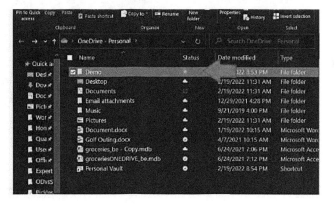

It is evident that the folder now displays a green circle with a white checkmark icon, signifying that all the files in this folder have been downloaded to establish a copy on the PC.

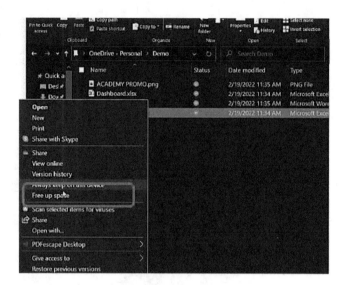

However, if you opt to right-click on any individual file within this folder and change its status to the cloud by selecting "Free up space," the folder icon will revert to displaying a cloud.

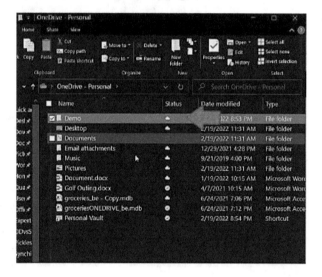

You also have the option to modify the syncing icon at the folder level

- Simply right-click on the folder and choose "Always keep on this device." This action will ensure that all files within this folder exist on both the PC and in the cloud.

- To alter the syncing status at the folder level, right-click on the folder and choose "Free up space." This action will transform the folder icon to a cloud, relocating all files in the folder to reside exclusively in the cloud.

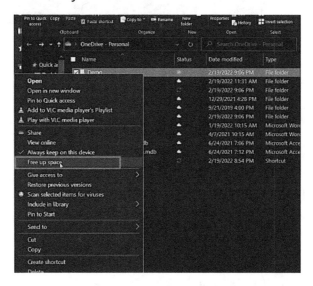

This is the method by which you can choose to have certain files exclusively on the cloud or have them available on both the PC and the cloud, both at the file and folder levels.

Distinguishing Between Green Check and White Check

As you navigate through your files on OneDrive, you may have come across a white circle with a green check icon.

It's crucial to note the distinction between the two checkmark icons:

- Files designated as "Always keep on this device" feature a green circle with a white check mark.
- Files marked as "Available on this device but can be offloaded using SourceSafe" are identified by a white circle with a green check mark.

Checking File Size

To observe the file size on both the PC and the cloud, adhere to the instructions below:

a. **On PC**
   - Right-click on the demo folder.
   - Choose Properties.
   - Navigate to "Size on Disk" to ascertain the folder size.

b. **Cloud**
   - Right-click on the demo folder.
   - Access Details.
   - Scroll down to review the file size.

Adding Files to PC and Cloud

Let's introduce a new file to OneDrive online and subsequently synchronize it with Microsoft OneDrive to view it on the PC:

- Open OneDrive online.
- Navigate to New > Excel Workbook for example
- Rename it as TestWorkbook, close the workbook, and refresh OneDrive. The new file will now be visible.
- Next, open OneDrive on your PC. If the file isn't present, initiate Microsoft OneDrive syncing.
- Navigate to the OneDrive icon on the taskbar below. Observe that syncing is currently paused. Click on it to resume syncing.
- Now, examine the OneDrive folder on your PC. You should locate the Test – Workbook there.

Likewise, you can add a file to your OneDrive folder on your PC and access it online.

- Simply right-click and choose New > Text Document.
- Rename the document as Test - Document.
- Refresh OneDrive online.
- This will trigger Microsoft OneDrive syncing, and you'll observe the document online as well.

We've discussed various syncing icons like the green check, white check, and cloud icons. Additionally, we've explored distinctions between file-level sync and folder-level sync.

Finally, we've covered how to compare file sizes on your PC versus the cloud and add a new file to both your PC and the cloud.

This article aims to illuminate the process of syncing with Microsoft OneDrive and understand the significance of different syncing icons. Now, you can efficiently utilize OneDrive. Feel free to revisit for a refresher on the basics!

CHAPTER FOUR

USING ONEDRIVE MOBILE ON YOUR PHONE

Guidelines for Installing and Setting Up Microsoft OneDrive on Android Phone/Tablet

- Open the "Play Store" on your Android device.

- In the search box, type "OneDrive" and select the official "OneDrive" app.

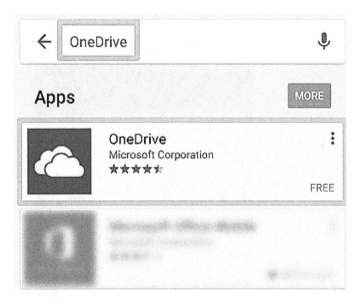

- Tap "Install" to download and install the app.

- Tap "Accept" to proceed with the installation.

- Once installed, open the "OneDrive" app.
- Select "Sign in now."

- Enter your email address in the format of "vtrv@hku.hk" and click onedrive_android_07.

- Enter your HKU Portal PIN in the password field and click "Sign in."

- You can now begin using OneDrive.

If you have multiple OneDrive accounts registered with Microsoft, sign in with the corresponding email address for the account you want to access. Each OneDrive account operates independently, and its contents are not shared among different accounts, even if registered under the same person. Exercise caution when signing in to OneDrive to avoid accessing the wrong account.

SCANNING WITH YOUR MOBILE APP

How to scan documents directly to OneDrive

If your job role includes document management, a significant aspect of your role likely revolves around scanning documents and preserving their digital versions as PDFs. This process can become laborious, especially when dealing with a substantial volume of documents using a cumbersome scanning machine. To streamline this task, save time, and conserve energy, consider utilizing OneDrive's document scanning feature. Learn more about how to scan directly to OneDrive for increased efficiency.

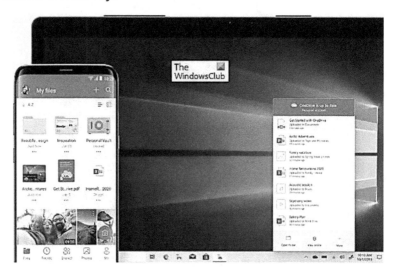

OneDrive Document Scanning Feature Explained

One of the primary functionalities of OneDrive's document scanning is the ability to use your mobile device to scan documents and save them as PDFs directly on OneDrive. This eliminates the need to scan documents with a traditional scanner, convert them into PDFs on your computer, and then transfer them to OneDrive, thereby saving valuable time.

Here are some noteworthy features of OneDrive document scanning:

- The OneDrive Mobile app is equipped with document scanning capabilities, eliminating the need for an additional scanning machine.
- Using a handheld scanner is straightforward – simply tap on the camera icon in the OneDrive mobile app and scan the document.
- The app allows you to scan and convert various items, such as paper documents, whiteboard notes, and receipts, into PDF files.
- OneDrive's folder system facilitates easy organization of scanned documents, enabling direct saving to OneDrive and access from any device.
- Archive important documents and even items like your child's artwork by converting them into PDF format.
- Edit scanned files by incorporating notes and drawings. OneDrive's markup tool allows you to add annotations, highlighted text, drawings, shapes, and symbols to scanned images and documents.
- Sharing scanned documents via email or with other users is a seamless process with the OneDrive document scanning feature.

How to Scan and Directly Save Documents to OneDrive

To utilize the OneDrive document scanning feature, ensure you meet the following prerequisites:

1. A Microsoft account for OneDrive access.
2. OneDrive installed on your PC (Note: If you have Windows 10 or a newer version, OneDrive is likely already installed by default).
3. The OneDrive application is installed on your mobile device.

Once these requirements are met, you can begin using document scanning and save directly to OneDrive.

Steps for Scanning and Saving a Document with OneDrive Document Scanning:

Follow these steps to scan a document and save it directly to OneDrive.

Scan the Document

Scanning a document using the OneDrive mobile app is as simple as taking a photo.

- Open the OneDrive app on your mobile device.
- Tap on the camera icon located at the lower bottom.

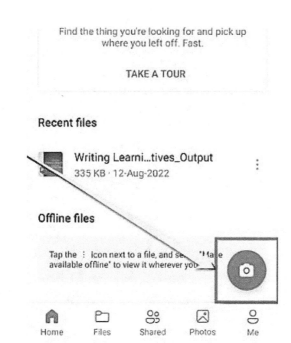

Find the thing you're looking for and pick up
where you left off. Fast.

TAKE A TOUR

Recent files

Writing Learni...tives_Output
335 KB · 12-Aug-2022

Offline files

Tap the ⋮ icon next to a file, and se... "Make
available offline" to view it wherever you...

Home   Files   Shared   Photos   Me

- This activates the camera app on your mobile device. (Ensure that you grant OneDrive permission to access your camera app). At this point, you'll encounter several scan options such as Whiteboard, Document, Business card, and Photo. Choose the appropriate option depending on the type of document you intend to scan.

- Now, press the white circle to initiate the document scan.

Edit (or Markup) the Scanned Document/Image

- The scanned document image will be displayed on the screen, accompanied by editing options at the bottom.

- By default, you can apply filters and perform actions such as cropping or rotating the image. To access more editing features, tap on the three dots located above the word "More." This will reveal additional options.

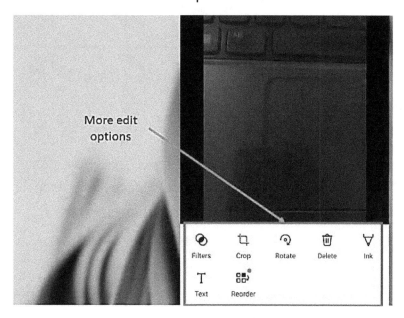

- Apply the desired effects and edit the image according to your needs. If the image doesn't meet your expectations, you can even delete it.
- After completing the editing process, tap on the "Done" button.

Save the Scanned Document on OneDrive

- The OneDrive app will prompt you to save the file. On the "Save As" screen, provide a new name for the scanned image and choose the location to save the file.

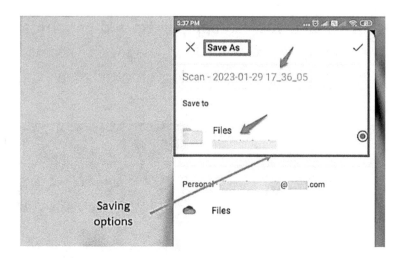

Saving
options

- Once you've saved the scanned file, you can find it in your OneDrive files. This folder is accessible from other devices synced with the same Microsoft credentials.

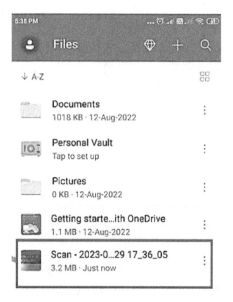

Beside the name of the scanned file, click on three vertical dots to access additional file options. From here, you can perform various actions such as sharing, deleting, downloading, copying, and more on this file.

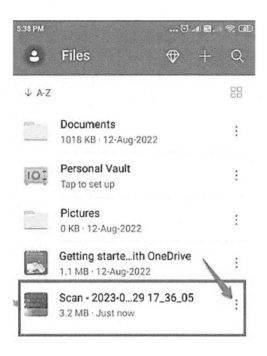

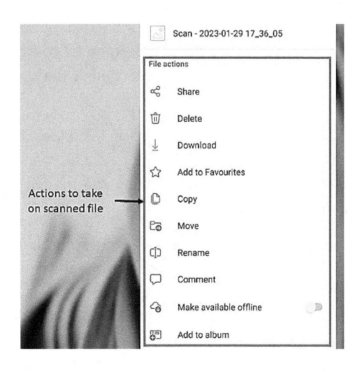

Actions to take on scanned file

CHAPTER FIVE

WHICH TOOLS FOR FILES: SHAREPOINT OR OneDrive

Since its inception in 2001, Microsoft SharePoint has evolved into a pivotal platform for collaborative business operations. Through successive versions, Microsoft has consistently refined SharePoint to meet the changing needs of businesses and individuals. This journey of evolution has seen enhancements in features, user interfaces, and performance capabilities.

From SharePoint 2001 to 2019, the platform has progressed from basic document management and search functionalities to the integration of cloud features like Power Apps, Power BI, and Power Automate in SharePoint 2019. The introduction of SharePoint Server Subscription Edition in March 2023 marked a milestone by consolidating monthly updates into a single package, streamlining the update process for enhanced security and features.

SharePoint Online, an integral part of Microsoft 365 subscriptions, offers distinct features, a different payment model, and seamless accessibility from anywhere, reflecting the modern trend of cloud-based collaboration tools.

In the dynamic digital landscape, keeping pace with the latest software versions is essential for optimal performance and security. The evolution of SharePoint, as outlined above, showcases the commitment to improvement. The Subscription Edition stands as the latest on-premises version, succeeding SharePoint Server 2019, and provides a direct upgrade path from both SharePoint 2019 and SharePoint 2016.

For those preferring an on-premises solution, SharePoint Server 2019 remains a robust choice. It incorporates cloud features to connect with on-premises data, making it an ideal platform for organizations not yet ready to transition to a subscription model. As SharePoint continues to adapt and innovate, it remains a versatile solution catering to a spectrum of organizational needs.

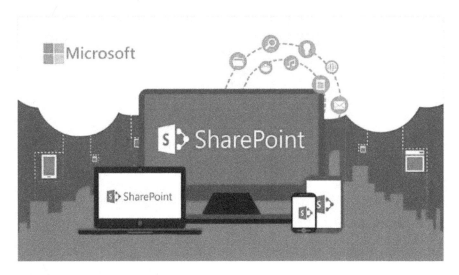

THE SIMILARITIES

Both platforms offer version history and co-authoring capabilities. In terms of security control, SharePoint adopts centralized control, allowing administrators to assign restricted permissions to specific users. Conversely, OneDrive mandates individual management of permissions.

THE DIFFERENCE

The ongoing debate on optimal storage solutions and the distinctions between various platforms persist. Today, we juxtapose two such mediums, shedding light on their disparities and commonalities.

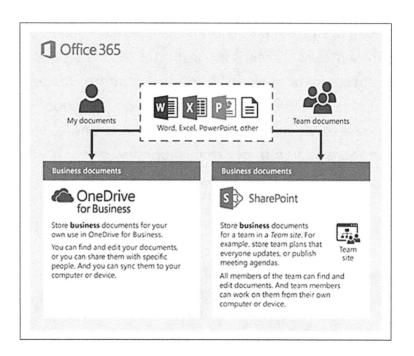

SharePoint, a web-based platform developed by Microsoft, serves as a multifaceted tool for document management, collaboration, and content organization within organizational frameworks. Acting as a central hub, SharePoint facilitates the storage, organization, and sharing of files, documents, and information among teams or throughout the entire organization.

On the other hand, OneDrive, Microsoft's cloud-based file hosting and synchronization service, allows users to store and share diverse data types, including files, photos, and documents, in the cloud. Accessible from various devices such as computers, tablets, and smartphones, OneDrive offers personal storage unless users opt to share permissions.

SharePoint determines access based on folder permissions, emphasizing collaborative sharing, while OneDrive primarily functions as personal storage unless explicit sharing permissions are granted. SharePoint is tailored for collaborative file sharing, while OneDrive is designed for drafting documents and sharing personal files.

SharePoint encompasses a diverse array of tools, including databases, libraries, calendars, and branding tools. In contrast, OneDrive serves as a file storage and sharing tool exclusively.

In conclusion, SharePoint emerges as an effective collaboration tool, fostering interaction among users across various departments within an organization. It facilitates the sharing of files, news, and content, streamlining processes and enhancing productivity. On the flip side, OneDrive is positioned as a personal file storage and sharing tool, primarily tailored for individual use and less suitable for extensive collaboration efforts.

SharePoint	OneDrive
Microsoft's original workspace that lets you create and share content, knowledge, and applications across organizations.	Microsoft's cloud storage and synchronization service that stores all your files securely in one place.
A site owner has full control privileges to the given SharePoint site.	Only the owner has the access rights to view, edit, or share the content.
SharePoint is a cloud storage solution that connects users to the Office suite.	OneDrive is a cloud-based storage solution for your personal files.
Capabilities extend beyond document sharing and collaboration.	OneDrive is like a personal space for private files.

D3 Difference Between.net

THE USE SHAREPOINT AND OneDrive

What Advantages Does Onedrive Offer

OneDrive simplifies the storage, access, and sharing of documents, photos, and files across multiple devices. Integrated with Office 365, it ensures users can access their files from anywhere, even enabling offline access through file synchronization across devices. With 5GB of free storage, users can store and retrieve files without additional costs.

The security and privacy of OneDrive are notable benefits

Users have control over file access, with features like two-factor authentication and encryption ensuring secure storage. OneDrive also supports file recovery, allowing users to restore accidentally deleted files.

Advantages of SharePoint

SharePoint serves as a secure collaborative platform for storing, organizing, and accessing information across devices within organizations. It facilitates team collaboration on various projects, including document creation, editing, list and calendar creation, and task tracking. SharePoint enables document and file sharing, providing access to a centralized information repository.

Custom workflow creation is a key advantage, streamlining processes and enhancing productivity. Users can customize the site's appearance, integrate with Microsoft applications like Outlook and Excel, and create custom forms to collect information securely.

Choosing Between OneDrive and SharePoint

The choice between OneDrive and SharePoint depends on specific needs. For personal file storage, photos, and documents, OneDrive is suitable. Integrated with Office 365 and offering 5GB of free storage, it ensures secure file access control.

For collaborative projects, custom workflows, and centralized information access, SharePoint is preferable. It supports document and file sharing, customizing site appearance, integration with Microsoft applications, and creating custom forms for secure data collection.

Security Features of OneDrive

OneDrive incorporates several security features to safeguard files and documents. Users control file access, and security measures like two-factor authentication and encryption are implemented. Users can recover deleted files and set passwords for shared links, restricting access through expiration dates and IP address restrictions.

Security Features of SharePoint

SharePoint provides robust security features, allowing users to control file access, implement two-factor authentication, and set expiration dates for shared links. Users can manage viewing, editing, and deletion permissions for documents, grant or revoke access, and restrict access to specific IP addresses. Additionally, users can set detailed permissions for files, controlling viewing, editing, and deletion rights.

Distinguishing Between Storing Files in OneDrive and SharePoint

In the realm of cloud storage and collaboration, both OneDrive and SharePoint stand out as excellent choices. Each platform boasts distinctive features and capabilities, necessitating a careful consideration of their respective pros and cons. OneDrive excels in straightforward storage and file-sharing functionalities, whereas SharePoint offers a more extensive suite of features, encompassing workflow automation and document management. Ultimately, the decision between OneDrive and SharePoint hinges on the user's specific needs and objectives.

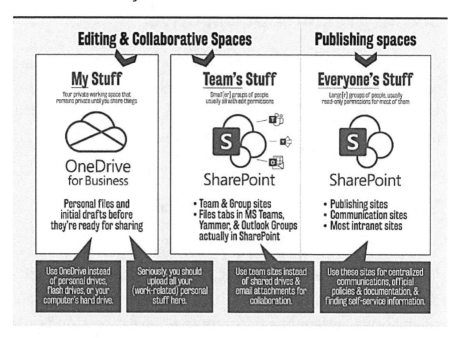

The Document Circle

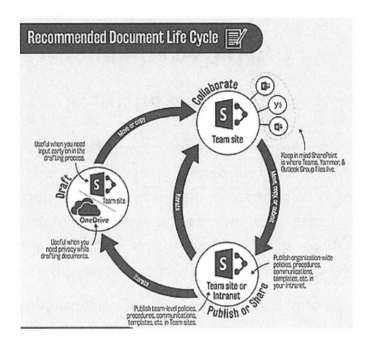

CHAPTER SIX

ONEDRIVE FOR BUSINESS

WHAT IS OneDrive FOR BUSINESS

OneDrive for Business serves as a dependable ally, comparable to a local superhero but for data! It functions as a cloud storage solution that not only securely houses vital files and documents but also enables access from anywhere, at any time. Designed specifically for organizations, it acts as a dynamic platform facilitating seamless collaboration and file sharing among business users.

While you might be familiar with the personal version of OneDrive, OneDrive for Business takes it a step further. Tailored for enterprises, it offers an array of added features including advanced security measures, seamless integration with other Microsoft 365 applications, and the capacity to handle larger data volumes. Essentially, OneDrive for Business is the big sibling in the same family, equipped with additional tools for the heavier demands of the business world.

Cloud Storage and Supercharged Cloud Storage

OneDrive for Business is not just ordinary storage; it's supercharged cloud storage. This is because the scale at which enterprises operate demands more than mere data storage. It empowers team members to access, collaborate, share, co-author, and perform various tasks with data stored in the cloud.

Storage Capacity of OneDrive for Business

OneDrive for Business provides 1 TB (terabyte) of storage per user as part of Microsoft 365's standard plans. For organizations with a minimum of five users on a qualifying plan, if a user's OneDrive for Business library reaches at least 90% of the 1 TB base storage allocation, the organization can increase the storage space up to 5 TB per user. For storage needs beyond 5 TB, additional storage can be requested from Microsoft.

Integration into Microsoft 365 Ecosystem

OneDrive for Business seamlessly integrates into the Microsoft 365 ecosystem, collaborating smoothly with services like Teams, SharePoint, and Office applications. This ensures files are readily accessible and editable where needed, simplifying workflows.

More Than a Tool

OneDrive for Business is not just a tool; it's a productivity booster. Advanced features such as co-authoring, version control, and data restoration minimize manual management, freeing up time for teams to focus on what truly matters. It leverages the power of the Microsoft 365 ecosystem to streamline operations and boost productivity.

If you're using OneDrive for Business, you can perform seamless Onedrive tenant-to-tenant migrations by following this comprehensive guide on how to migrate OneDrive from one tenant to another.

Unique Features of OneDrive for Business

Let's explore the distinctive features OneDrive for Business brings to the table:

- Beyond storage, it provides smart storage, enabling remote work without disrupting workflow
- Microsoft 365 usage analytics offer insights into data stored on OneDrive.
- Microsoft provides an extraordinary level of security with OneDrive for Business, safeguarding enterprise data in transit or at rest.
- Seamless integration with your device's File Explorer for easy viewing of OneDrive data.
- Syncing folders like Documents and Pictures with OneDrive to prevent data loss.
- Allows access to previous versions of files, simplifying collaboration.
- Enables multiple users to work on the same file simultaneously.
- Supports multinational companies in distributing storage among different regions.
- Keeps deleted data on the cloud for up to 30 days, allowing restoration.

Using OneDrive for Business for Collaboration

Beyond data storage, OneDrive for Business emphasizes collaboration, especially in sharing data inside and outside your organization. Here are key aspects to consider:

- Create shareable links for files with customizable permissions.
- Foundation for collaboration, accessible across Microsoft Teams, SharePoint, and Outlook.

- Useful for external collaborators to ensure data availability for a limited period.
- Limit specific individuals from accessing data by adjusting external sharing settings.
- Create security groups to control access to sensitive content.
- Policies to restrict data access are crucial for highly regulated companies.
- Admins can limit data access to devices compliant with company policies, enhancing security.

Where files are stored in OneDrive for Business

On the cloud, naturally. Once you log in to OneDrive, you'll have direct visibility to all your files.

Note: Files shared via Microsoft Teams chat automatically find a home in the "Microsoft Teams Chat Files" folder within OneDrive.

A centralized hub for accessible data storage That's correct. OneDrive for Business serves as a central repository for organizing all your organization's data, fostering smoother collaboration. Employees can swiftly and conveniently access files because they know precisely where to find them.

Files can be categorized, and subfolders can establish hierarchies to structure data. For instance, a company might store all its files on OneDrive, with each folder denoting a distinct department—categories like "HR Department," "Accounts Department," "IT Department," and so on. If you're searching for the "Feb 2022 Payroll" file, chances are it's in the "Payroll" subfolder within the parent "Accounts Department" folder.

OneDrive for Business and Your File Server When considering file servers such as OneDrive and Microsoft 365, two scenarios emerge:

Scenario 1: File servers are generally an on-premises affair. If your data resides on a file server, you can collaborate within a private on-premises network, but your data stays off the cloud. You have the option to migrate your file server data to OneDrive, transitioning from on-premises to the cloud.

Scenario 2: Another scenario involves data stored on SharePoint, technically categorized as a server file. An advantage of server files on a SharePoint site is that the data isn't tied to any user; the business owns it.

For clarity, consider the example of file servers and SharePoint. Imagine Jim uploads critical data to OneDrive. All goes well; Jim grants access to other team members, and collaboration flourishes. However, if Jim decides to leave the company, deleting his account poses a dilemma. All the data Jim uploaded would be lost. But if the data were on SharePoint, the server file would remain unaffected, detached from any user account deletions.

DOWNLOADING ALL FILES FROM ONEDRIVE FOR BUSINESS

Retrieve All Files and Folders from OneDrive for Business via Web Browser Utilizing Microsoft's

OneDrive for Business offers an excellent means of storing and collaborating on files. However, if the need arises to obtain a comprehensive download of all files within your OneDrive for Business account, I'll guide you on how to accomplish this task.

- Sign in to your OneDrive site using the URL shortcut: https://YourDomain-My.sharepoint.com/ (or access another user's OneDrive site if you have the necessary permissions – if not, follow the steps in "How to Get Access to OneDrive for Business Site of Other Users?").
- Choose all the desired files and folders, then click the "Download" button on the toolbar.

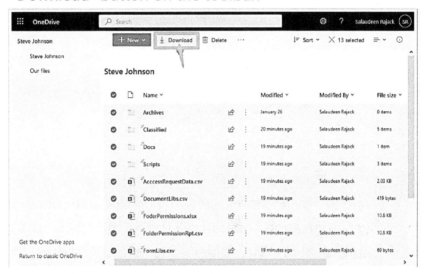

This will initiate the download of everything from the OneDrive site into a Zip file on your local PC.

Using Sync Option

Download all files from the OneDrive for Business site using the Sync Option Allow me to demonstrate how to download all your files from OneDrive, creating a local copy on your computer through the Sync option. This ensures constant access to your files, even in the event of issues with OneDrive or your internet connection.

- Navigate to the OneDrive site from which you wish to download files.

- Click on the "Sync" button in the toolbar (Ensure the OneDrive client is installed on your local machine). This will commence the synchronization process from OneDrive to your local disk.

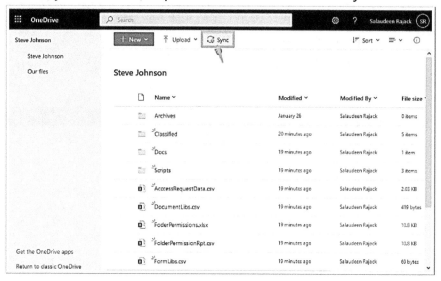

- Launch File Explorer, find the folder generated through the synchronization operation under the "YourDomain" node, right-click on the folder, and select "Always keep on this device." This action initiates the download of all content from OneDrive, rather than merely establishing the synchronization link.

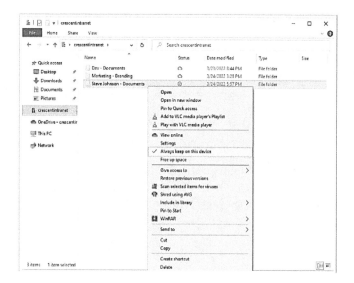

ORGANIZING YOUR PHOTOS AND VIDEOS

To effectively arrange your photos and videos in OneDrive for Business, leverage features like photo search and albums. Once your photos are uploaded, easily locate them in the All Photos view, where images captured on the same date are grouped together. You have the option to craft personalized albums by navigating to Photos > Albums > New album, assigning a name, and subsequently adding photos through the "Add album" feature.

Additionally, you can refine your organization by editing or removing automatically generated tags by OneDrive. Simply select a photo, choose "Edit tags," and either input a new tag or click the 'x' next to an existing tag for removal. While OneDrive doesn't generate albums automatically, you can manually assemble albums for streamlined sharing with friends or family.

Should you desire a more structured approach with columns and views, access the OneDrive for Business library. Click "Return to classic OneDrive" in the lower left corner, and within the library ribbon, establish columns and views to efficiently filter items based on specific criteria. This can significantly enhance the organization and accessibility of your files. I trust this guidance proves beneficial!

RECOVERING A LOST FILE OR DOCUMENT IN ONEDRIVE

OneDrive files are no longer visible

If specific files are absent from your OneDrive folder, there's a possibility they were inadvertently deleted. To recover them, check the Recycle Bin on OneDrive. Keep in mind that protected items may not be directly visible within the OneDrive folder. Additionally, consider whether you've enabled Files On Demand or if only specific folders are being synced, as this could impact file visibility.

Issues such as app corruption or interruptions during the backup process may also contribute to files going missing.

If you're facing OneDrive files missing from the folder, utilize the following methods to recover your data:

- Manually search for missing files on OneDrive Live.
- Check for missing files in the OneDrive Recycle Bin.
- Examine the Personal Vault folder on OneDrive Live.
- Initiate a manual start of the OneDrive backup.
- Adjust Indexing Options.
- Reset OneDrive.
- Consider using a data recovery tool.
- Reinstall OneDrive.

Begin by manually searching for missing files on OneDrive Live to address the issue.

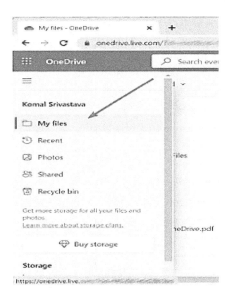

If you're unable to locate OneDrive files on your PC, consider searching for them on the OneDrive live website. A potential sync issue may be preventing OneDrive from saving files on your desktop, but the files might be securely stored on the live website associated with your account. To access these files:

- Navigate to the official OneDrive Live website using a web browser and log in to your Microsoft account.
- Select the "My files" tab from the left-side panel.
- The right-side pane will display all your files and folders.
- Utilize the Search box to enter the name of a missing file and verify its availability.

This approach allows you to check and retrieve missing files directly from the OneDrive live website.

As an additional step:

Examine the OneDrive Recycle Bin for missing files

It's possible that you inadvertently deleted certain files, leading to their absence in the OneDrive folder on your PC. If this situation applies, you can check the Recycle bin in your OneDrive to locate the missing files and folders. Follow these steps:

- Log in to your OneDrive Live account.
- Navigate to the "Recycle bin" tab on the left-side panel.
- In the right-side pane, you'll find a list of all deleted items.
- If the Recycle bin contains the files you're seeking, select those files and click the "Restore" button to recover them. Alternatively, you can use the "Restore all items" option.

Check the Personal Vault folder on OneDrive Live

The Personal Vault serves as a secure repository within OneDrive, safeguarding confidential and sensitive files and folders. If you're experiencing difficulty locating certain files, they may be stored within the Personal Vault folder, restricting immediate access. In such cases, follow these steps to check for the missing files:

- Open OneDrive Live and go to the "My files" tab on the left-side panel.
- Click on the "Personal Vault" folder in the right-side section. This action prompts identity verification.
- Select your email ID and a verification code will be sent to your email. Enter the code and click "Verify" to complete the verification process. You can now access the files and folders within the Personal Vault.

Manually Start OneDrive Backup

If the folder backup was interrupted or stopped unexpectedly, manually initiate the OneDrive backup for your folders. Right-click on your OneDrive folder, choose "OneDrive," and then select "Manage OneDrive backup." Choose the folders you wish to back up and press the "Start backup" button.

Change Indexing Options

If the search feature fails to locate OneDrive files and folders, it may be due to the OneDrive folder being excluded from indexing. To address this, follow these steps:

- Open Windows Search, type "Indexing Options," and select the top result.
- Click on the "Modify" button.
- In the dialog window, locate your username and check the box next to the OneDrive folder.
- Press "OK" to save the changes.

By completing these steps, you can potentially resolve issues related to missing files in the Personal Vault, initiate manual OneDrive backup, and adjust indexing options for effective file search.

Reset OneDrive

If OneDrive encounters issues syncing your files and folders, and you're unable to access files on your computer, consider resetting OneDrive to resolve the problem. Follow these steps:

- Open the Run command box using Win+R.

- Enter the following command in the Open field: **%localappdata%\Microsoft\OneDrive\onedrive.exe /reset**.

- Allow a few minutes for OneDrive to reset.

- Reopen Run and enter the command: **%localappdata%\Microsoft\OneDrive\onedrive.exe**.

- Check if the issue is resolved.

Use a Data Recovery Tool

Explore the option of using a data recovery tool to retrieve lost data from the OneDrive folder. There are effective tools like WinfrGUI, FreeUndelete, and others available for Windows. Test whether you can recover missing files using any of these tools.

Reinstall OneDrive

If the problem persists, and you cannot locate certain files in OneDrive, your OneDrive app may be corrupted. In this case, uninstall and then reinstall OneDrive on your computer. Verify if this resolves the issue.

USING THE SKYPE FOR A BUSINESS PLATFORM

Skype for Business Setup Guides

Skype for Business, an instant messaging and video chat application, is an integral part of Office 365 for students. This platform facilitates communication with fellow students and the organization of online meetings through the calendar feature. Skype for Business can be utilized through web access, on desktop computers, or on mobile devices.

For online access

- Log in to myoffice.ivey.ca.
- Navigate to "Apps" and open Outlook.
- Click the Skype icon located in the top navigation bar, adjacent to the Notifications and Settings icons. This action will launch Skype for Business.

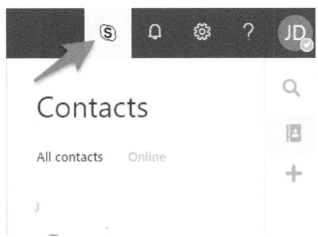

Viewing your contacts, searching for people at Ivey, or initiating a new conversation and adding participants is easily accomplished in Skype for Business. Here's how to set up and access the application on both desktop and mobile devices:

On Desktop

Visit the Microsoft Office Desktop Setup Guide for comprehensive instructions on installing the latest Microsoft Office suite, which includes Skype for Business. If you prefer to install only Skype for Business without the other Office 365 applications, follow these steps:

- Log in to myoffice.ivey.ca and click "Install Office apps" on the home page.
- Select "Other install options."

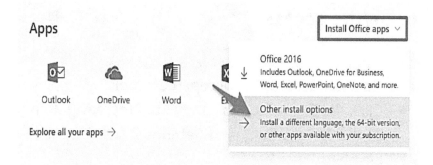

- On the ensuing page listing Office 365 applications, navigate to "Software" in the left navigation and click "Skype for Business."

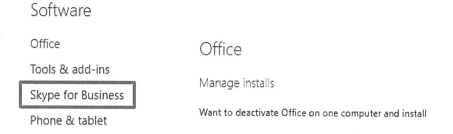

- For full functionality, click "Install" under Skype for Business 2024
- Download the installation file, run it, and follow the on-screen steps.

Once installed, open Skype for Business, sign in with your Ivey email and password and start using the application.

For additional information on Skype for Business, including instructions on adjusting audio and video settings, refer to the Microsoft support site.

On Your Mobile Device: To access Skype for Business on your mobile device, download the Skype for Business app from the Google Play Store or the iOS App Store. Follow these steps:

- Open the Skype for Business app and select Advanced Options.

- Turn off the Auto-Detect Server and input webdir.online.lync.com for both the Internal Discovery Address and External Discovery Address.
- Enter your Ivey email address and select "X" in the top right corner.
- Input your Ivey email address in the Organization Sign-In Address and select the Forward Arrow.
- Enter your Ivey password on the Ivey login page (SSO).
- Provide your mobile phone number for joining Skype for Business meetings.
- Navigate through any additional prompts based on your preferences. Accept the licensing agreement if prompted.

CHAPTER SEVEN

MICROSFT ONEDRIVE TOP TIPS AND TRICKS

OneDrive stands out as an efficient cloud storage and synchronization solution provided by Microsoft. It seamlessly uploads your files to the cloud, granting you the flexibility to retrieve them from any location. Additionally, OneDrive facilitates file sharing and real-time collaboration with others. Despite its robust capabilities, many users only scratch the surface of what OneDrive can offer. To unlock its full potential, we're here to present the top 9 tips and tricks for leveraging all the features that come with this service.

Optimize Your OneDrive Experience with These Top 9 Tips:

Whether you're collaborating with others or efficiently managing your storage, these tips are essential for maximizing the benefits of Microsoft OneDrive.

Establish a Bidirectional Connection Between OneDrive and Your Local Storage

Utilize OneDrive's Folder Backup feature to securely back up your local computer files to the cloud, ensuring data recovery in the event of a crash or accidental deletion.

Similarly, OneDrive's Sync feature maintains a local copy of your cloud files, offering swift access and guaranteeing that they remain up-to-date.

Together, these features form a two-way bridge connecting your OneDrive and personal computer. Configure them easily by following these steps:

- Click on the white or blue OneDrive icon in the Windows taskbar notification area.
- Select 'Settings' from the dropdown after clicking on the OneDrive Help and Settings icon.

- Follow the subsequent steps based on your specific requirements.

For PC Folder Backup		For Sync	
1	• Head over to the Backup Tab	• Head over to the Account Tab	
2	• Click on Manage Backup	• Click on Choose Folder	
3	• Choose the folders you back up	• Tick the folders you want to Sync	
4	• Click on Start Backup	• Hit OK	

Secure your email attachments on OneDrive

Transfer your email attachments to OneDrive effortlessly by configuring OneDrive to automatically save all attachments received in your Microsoft Outlook. This ensures you never lose an attachment again.

To integrate your Outlook with the OneDrive app, follow these straightforward steps using Microsoft Power Automate:

- Sign up for a Power Automate account.
- Click on the template named "Save Outlook.com attachments to your OneDrive," as indicated below, and follow the provided prompts.

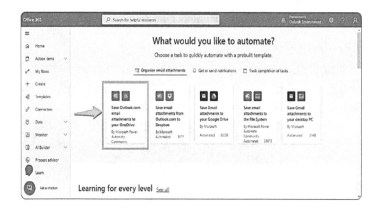

Synchronize Google Drive with OneDrive effortlessly

With approximately 800 million daily active users on Google Drive, chances are your client, partner, or freelancer colleague is already using it. Instead of requesting a switch to OneDrive, opt for syncing the two platforms. This ensures a seamless collaboration experience.

Integrately simplifies the process of connecting OneDrive to Google Drive. Through this integration, you can automate the transfer of your OneDrive files to Google Drive and vice versa. This ready-to-use, one-click automation handles it all for you! 👆

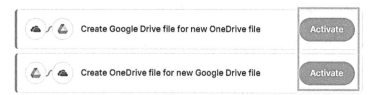

Furthermore, effortlessly link your OneDrive account with more than 1050+ apps through Integrated in just a few clicks. Don't hesitate! Stay ahead of the curve in your endeavors. Join us now and explore the myriad of powerful OneDrive integrations available.

Facilitate Real-time Collaboration and Secure Sharing with Link Expiration

When sharing a OneDrive file or folder, you now have the ability to:

- Specify who can access the link.
- Set the duration for which the link will remain active.

This feature proves invaluable when sharing sensitive information, allowing you to control the link's availability for a defined period. Easily manage access and expiration permissions by navigating to the "Share Link" settings, as illustrated below. Once the link expires, recipients can no longer access the shared file or folder.

Ensure Data Security and Recovery with Version History

In the event of accidental deletions or regrettable changes, OneDrive offers a comprehensive history of all file modifications. Follow these straightforward steps, either on the cloud or in your local storage, to recover previous file versions:

- Right-click on the desired file.
- Select 'Version History' from the dropdown.
- Right-click on the preferred version and choose 'Restore.'

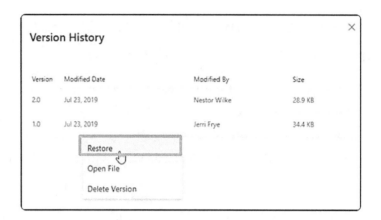

Access OneDrive files without utilizing local storage

Offline access and On-Demand files prove to be highly beneficial features of OneDrive. Nonetheless, it's crucial to grasp the distinction between the two options before choosing the most suitable one for your needs.

Offline Access files are downloaded and synchronized with your personal computer, enabling you to retrieve them even when offline.

On-demand files reside solely in the cloud and aren't downloaded to your personal computer. Nevertheless, you can conveniently access them through File Explorer on your computer when connected to the internet, streamlining your experience and eliminating the need to switch between applications.

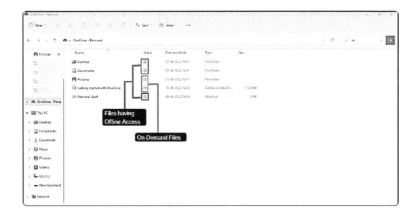

Files having
Offline Access

On-Demand Files

Access OneDrive on your mobile devices

When you require on-the-go access to your OneDrive files, there are several methods available:

- Install the OneDrive app on your Android or iOS device.
- Utilize the web interface through your mobile browser.

Connect with family and friends through Group Sharing

Enhance collaboration by adding team members working on the same project to a OneDrive Family. This facilitates the sharing of files with the entire group collectively, streamlining the process compared to individual file transfers. This approach ensures that everyone in the group has access to the shared files, keeping everyone on the same page with up-to-date information. Microsoft provides a helpful guide to get started with group sharing in OneDrive.

Enhance security with a Personal Vault

For added security when storing sensitive information in your OneDrive account, leverage the "Personal Vault" feature. This feature encrypts your files and mandates additional authentication before granting access, providing an extra layer of protection for your confidential data.

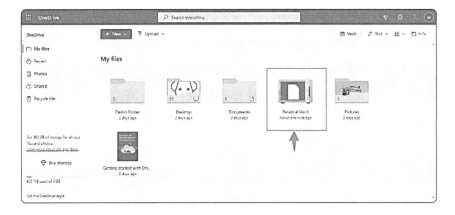

OneDrive will automatically lock your Personal Vault if it remains inactive for a specific period.

UPLOADING FROM YOUR PHONE'S CAMERA

Scan Documents

Sometimes, there's a need to swiftly scan and share various documents, such as:

- A signed contract or a paper form
- Whiteboards
- Receipts
- Academic/Professional transcripts
- Business cards, and more.

The OneDrive mobile app offers a convenient solution by allowing you to use your phone's camera for document scanning and uploading. You can easily crop, rotate, make adjustments, or even add your signature to the scanned document before sharing. This feature proves especially valuable when you're on the move and require a rapid scanning and sharing solution.

To utilize this functionality, follow these straightforward steps on your OneDrive mobile app:

1. Click on the Scan Icon in the OneDrive mobile app.
2. Select the document type.
3. Tap the white circle icon to initiate the scanning process.
4. Edit the image using the available editing tools.
5. Hit Done.
6. Name your file and click on Save.

CONCLUSION

OneDrive stands as a robust tool designed to streamline your life by providing convenient access to your files regardless of your location. Catering to both individuals and businesses, it boasts an array of features. With its exemplary security, user-friendly interface, and adaptability, OneDrive has rightfully earned its status as one of the most widely used cloud storage services today. To enhance your OneDrive experience even more, our tips offer numerous ways to leverage Microsoft OneDrive effectively. Give them a try and witness the seamless integration for yourself!

our Essential Guide to Effortless File Management and Troubleshooting" is a comprehensive handbook designed to empower users with the latest insights into Microsoft's OneDrive for Business. This succinct guide covers a range of crucial topics, from retrieving all files and folders seamlessly via web browsers and understanding the intricate storage architecture within OneDrive for Business to addressing issues such as app corruption and backup interruptions that may lead to file loss.

Readers will gain valuable insights into safeguarding their data by exploring the Personal Vault folder on OneDrive Live and maximizing collaboration through integration with the SKYP for Business platform. Additionally, the guide unveils "OneDrive 9 Top Tips and Tricks," offering expert advice to enhance efficiency, organization, and productivity within the OneDrive ecosystem. Stay ahead of the curve with the latest advancements in OneDrive technology by embracing the wisdom within "Mastering OneDrive 2024."

INDEX

B

Bidirectional, v, 65
Browser Offline Functionality, ii, 7

C

cloud storage, 1, 2, 3, 7, 45, 47, 64, 73
co-authoring mode, 3
Collaboration, ii, iv, v, 12, 50, 68
complimentary, 17
Copilot Integration, ii, 8
Custom workflow, 43

D

Data Recovery, v, 60
DESKTOP USER INTERFACE, ii, 4
Dropbox, 2, 4

E

Ecosystem, iv, 48

G

Green Check and White Check, iii, 24

H

hard drive, 3

I

icons, 9, 19, 24, 26, 61
incorporates, 5, 39, 44

L

Linux, ii, 15

M

Microsoft 365, iv, 5, 8, 39, 47, 48, 49, 51
modifications, 2, 5, 13, 17, 68

N

New Interface, ii, 5

O

OneDrive, ii, iii, iv, v, 1, 2, 3, 4, 5, 6, 7, 8, 9, 10, 12, 13, 14, 15, 16, 17, 18, 19, 20, 24, 25, 26, 27, 29, 30, 31, 32, 33, 36, 38, 40, 41, 42, 43, 44, 45, 47, 48, 49, 50, 51, 52, 53, 54, 55, 56, 57, 58, 59, 60, 64, 65, 66, 67, 68, 69, 70, 71, 72, 73, 74
ONEDRIVE, ii, iii, iv, v, 2, 4, 14, 17, 18, 27, 43, 47, 52, 55, 64
onedrive.com, 9

P

PCs, 3
Personal Vault, 58

S

SCANNING, iii, 30
SHAREPOINT, iii, iv, 38, 43
SKYP, v, 61, 74
Supercharged, iv, 47
synchronized, 2, 69
synchronizes, 2, 3
Synchronizing, ii, 13